MW00365196

How To Become A

Successful Young Woman

Mercedes Woodberry
Diamond D. McNulty

Copyright © 2016 McNulty International LLC

All rights reserved.

ISBN-13: 978-1945318016

ISBN-10: 1945318015

"Taking Over The World" – Diamond McNulty

Dedication:

This book is dedicated to every young woman walking the face of the earth. I love you, I'm proud of you and I look forward to seeing you all grow to become successful at all of your endeavors.

– Diamond McNulty

Acknowledgments

I'd like to thank my friend Ty Spears. Through everything you have unknowingly been my rock. When I call you always pick up and you're always there. Sometimes it's not about how you help people financially, but how you help people mentally and emotionally. Hard times reveal true friends and you have proven yourself to be my biggest supporter.

I'd also like to acknowledge a few women who provided priceless guidance to help me on my journey to success.

"Make Executive Decision Only"
- Ms. Cheba

"*When dealing with your Soldiers always be assertive but fair"***- Ms. Walker**

"Don't worry about what others say about you. People will always talk and you can't change that; you know who you are and that's what count."
- Ms. Mitchell

"You will make it through what has happened to you in your past, I am sure of this. No matter what I am always here if you need me." **- Ms. Mosequeda**

Thank you.

Special Thanks

I'd like to send a special thank you to a woman who has dedicated her life to helping girls across the world...Carrie Coleman. Carrie is a true leader with the passion to persevere and help others become better in every aspect of life. I'd also like to thank Freddie Chapel Wright and Kimberly Pearson for reviewing this book ahead of time and giving great feedback to help us make it perfect.

How this book became...

I was reading *How To Become A Successful Young Man* written by my older brother Diamond McNulty and throughout the entire reading I couldn't help but ask myself, "What about the young women who want guidance on how to become successful?"

Later that week I facetimed Diamond to provide him feedback on his book. During our conversation he mentioned he was working on the female version because the world was demanding it. I went on to tell Diamond that if there was a female in the world as driven and as successful as him then she could have written the book. Before I could move on to the next topic Diamond looked directly in the camera and stated, "There is a female version of me, and she's you sis."

My mind started racing with all the trials and tribulations that got me from where I started from to where I am today. Born into a poor family I lived in Chicago's Robert Taylor Projects and moved around a lot throughout my lifetime. I attended 12 different schools from 1st -12th grade, was expelled from middle school, became a runaway, a pregnant teenager and got arrested for felony theft all before age 18.

I want every young woman to understand that your current circumstances are not permanent and every obstacle you are facing is just that... an obstacle. Everyone can experience success and together we are here to help you on your journey.

Beauty Is Her Name

By: Diamond McNulty

I am Beautiful! I am unique!

I'm not what others want me to be

I have style, I have dreams

I have big goals to achieve

I am strong… I'm a gem

I will value who I am

More than silver, more than gold

My mother's child has broken the mold

I'm a priceless piece of Art

I will set myself apart

I will not slow or fit in
I was truly born to win

When my husband notices me
Butterflies is what I see

Roses of love will fill the air
When I walk they stop and stare

From the texture of my hair
To the clothes I like to wear

I can do anything… yes I can
They respect me as I am

I stand strong and I can bend
I'm a beautiful woman

TABLE OF CONTENTS

PREFACE

"Success doesn't count unless you earn it fair and square." – **Michelle Obama**

LOOK AROUND YOU!

How many young women your age are reading this book? Not many. You have already taken the first step to success. Once you turn 16 years old or older, you have to understand that you are no longer a kid and you should be thinking seriously about what you want to be in life. If you missed what I said, here is the previous line once more...

"Once you turn 16 years old, you have to

understand that you are no longer a kid and you should be thinking seriously about what you want to be in life". This is when you come up with your success plan.

For young women, by the age of 16, you are at the beginning stages of womanhood.

This point is critical because you have to develop your mind into thinking like an adult while still being looked at as a child. The decisions you make from this moment forward will show how responsible or irresponsible you are.

Your reputation for being responsible begins now, and believe me being responsible is

<u>very important</u>.

In this book we plan on providing you with fundamental information for becoming successful but it is completely up to you to build the prosperity. Let's begin!

CHAPTER 1

You Are Beautiful

Beautiful: Having beauty; possessing qualities that give great pleasure or satisfaction to see, hear, think about, etc.

Being beautiful is made up of three categories combined. What we **see**, what we **hear**, and what we **think**. When we look in the mirror "we see" and when "we hear" others opinions "we think". What do we think about? Right, you guess it, how beautiful we are.

We were all born with different features that make up the "beauty" we are. From our hair colors/textures, eye colors, outer skin tones all the way to our inner spirit. In society one might even classify height and weight as a form of beauty but let's be real... from head to toe everyone is different.

Different: (Unique) is a beautiful word that means not alike in character or quality; distinct in nature; dissimilar.

In order to realize your true beauty, you must first embrace being different. You are not like anyone else in character or quality. I love it... the best feeling in the world is knowing that I am me and no one else can be me. Wouldn't you agree?

If someone was 100% like you wouldn't it be kind of annoying? Since you were born in your own skin start today and enhance your own beauty by falling in love with you.

Looking back in history there are huge companies that have made billions of dollars utilizing the <u>insecurities of a woman's beauty</u>.

Insecurities: The uncertainty about oneself; lack of confidence.

Many of the things we think are flaws which make us insecure, are truly beauty marks that enhance who we are and solidify our differences.

As a young woman in today's world we use all types of things to <u>cover up</u> our natural beauty. Take a look -

- Eye Shadow
- Eye Liner

- Mascara
- Lip Gloss
- Lip Color
- Concealer
- Bronzer
- Make-up
- Beauty Products
- Cosmetics

However, all of these products above are ok to use from time to time because as young women we love to get dolled up. But understand, there is a difference between getting dolled up for a special event and covering up what we or others
see as flaws that make us feel insecure. I remember the time when only my grandmother wore fake hair/wigs and now

everyone is wearing them covering up who they are as young as 7 years old.

Question: What happens when you get home and have to take off all those things that are covering you up? What happens if you find someone who you like and they like who you are while you're covered up, and as soon as you uncover who you are, they stop liking you? Some men often refer to this as "false advertising". Embracing your natural beauty will show how strong and confident you are. Fall in love with yourself and others will fall in love with you as well.

Quick Tip:

The best feeling in the world is for someone to love you for whom you are... Naturally.

Fall In Love With You

You are beautiful, I know this, but do you know this? Your success depends on your confidence in you. Confidence comes from looking at and inside yourself and believing that you are mentally and physically brilliant.

As women we tend to be really hard on ourselves in regards to our physical beauty. **One way to change this mindset -** Do not compare yourself to the woman on the screen. When you look at a magazine, see a music video, or a movie do not compare yourself to the woman on the screen.

Setup to Fail. We set ourselves up for failure when we compare ourselves to unrealistic standards of beauty. Every other year there is a new trend that everyone is jumping on from implant enhancements to materialistic purchases, etc. **What happens when it all goes out of style?** It's time to throw everything away and start all over. If you blend in with the trends you will go out of style eventually as well. You don't want blend in, you want to be the trendsetter and the only way to do that is by creating your own style.

Many of us have personal insecurities even if no one else notices them we do... big nose, thin hair, big ears or my personal one a big forehead. It's not about the insecurity it is about how you carry yourself and the confidence of not letting that insecurity define you. The media wants you to cover up your flaws by caking on make-up, getting weaves, and buying useless items because it makes them richer and sells you the dream of making you "glamorous".

Note: *There is a difference between glam and beauty, glam is purchased and beauty comes naturally. From this point forward do not compare yourself to celebrities or random people on the screen because their glam does not compare to your beauty.*

– Mercedes Woodberry.

It's Ok To Be Smart

> **Smart**: Having or showing quick intelligence or ready mental capability.

Growing up we have all seen the so called "nerds" get picked on for their intelligent abilities to comprehend and apply the materials being taught to them. We also see the "average" students joking around using school as a social hour rather than a time to learn. Looking at the difference, ask yourself... **How can being smart be a bad thing?** All of the people who are very successful in the world embrace their abilities and use them to achieve greatness. It is very important that you take full advantage of all educational opportunities, so that in the future when you enter into certain doors or surround yourself with certain people, what you know will allow you to prosper. Knowledge is the key to success when applied.

Example: If you want to choose Acting as a career, education plays a huge part. What happens after you get that position you've been looking for but can't <u>read</u> the script or understand the contract you're signing. You will and can be easily taken advantage of.

Degrees can make you marketable, however self-educating in your passion can also help you excel in life. Once I figured out this secret I stayed three steps ahead of everyone, by reading biographies of successful people and learning from their mistakes. In doing this for yourself, it will provide you the ability to become better than which they were.

Emotions

As women we were built with a natural instinct to care, love and nurture the things around us. Our emotional being is something that we cannot fully control for it is a natural part of being a woman due to our estrogen production. Embrace, understand

and turn it into a positive and beneficial characteristic.

Sometimes as we get promoted, reach for the stars and strive to pursue our dreams in life we feel as if we must hide our feminine side to show that we are strong. Be yourself: your mannerism, feelings, and thoughts are what make you who you are. However, it's your <u>knowledge</u> and <u>verbal communication</u> that will lead you to victory. Some men are physically stronger than women but that doesn't mean you can't compete with them. Be yourself, your emotions can bring a lot of good to the table. Control your emotions in a professional manner because nce you become the President, CEO or Command Sergeant Major, your employees will expect nothing less than <u>professional leadership</u>.

Short Story

I worked at a McDonalds not too far from my house, but one night I wanted to hang out with a girlfriend. I called in sick to work and went to her house. This was completely innocent. Jasmine was 15 (and I was 16) and her mom was home. She cooked us spaghetti. We watched movies and talked about the JROTC drill team competition we had the following morning.

My mom called my job and the manager told her I was not there. My mom called me and asked me where I was and I responded, "at work." She told me she called my job and to bring my you know what home and she related that I was probably at a boy's house being fast.

I became overwhelmed with fear,

anxiety, but most importantly anger. I was angrier than fearful because my mom told me I was at a boy's house being, "fast." I asked Jasmine's mom if I could just stay for the night and she told me no, that was kidnapping.

So what did I do? I got in my beat up Dodge Stratus and hopped on I-10 headed to Georgia. At this time, we were living in Louisiana, but I had close friends in Georgia that I knew would let me stay the night or two.

I'm crying while I'm driving, I'm hitting the steering wheel, my mom was blowing up my phone with threatening text message and voice mails, but I was determined to get to Georgia. All these emotions were running through my body. I did not know how long I had been driving, but then my heart skipped a beat when I read the sign "Welcome to Texas, The Lone Star State." I was going the wrong way the entire time.

Being that it was so late, I just parked at a hotel and slept in the car. I woke up the next morning and decided to head back to Louisiana and face the music. As I was driving my tire blew out on the interstate and I had no spare. Emotions took over my body once again and I began shaking at this point. I get out the car and accept the fact that I am about to die... my only choice was to hitch hike. Here I am 5'0", 115lbs on the interstate with my thumb out, crying, broke, mad, and willing to get in anyone's car who was willing to stop.

Ultimately, a mother and daughter stopped, picked me up, and took me to a spare tire place. The mom bought me a spare tire, took me back to my car, changed my tire, gave me $20, their phone number, and trailed me half way home.

Moral of the Story: The way I handled my emotions in that 24-hour period could have killed me. Have emotions, but express them and act in a professional and reasonable manner as much as possible.

NOTES

1/7/18

I Love my skin and my heart.

Tahira

CHAPTER 1 REVIEW

1. Define Beautiful?

Beautiful Mean you are Beautiful
in the in side those mean on
the outside.

2. Do not compare yourself to

to other people
_____.

3. It's Ok to Be biffernt.

4. Glam is purchased but beauty comes

the inside.

CHAPTER 2

When I Grow Up

When thinking about your life and growing up, you should ask yourself <u>3</u>-questions?

When answering these three questions I want you to be bold and reach for the stars! Don't limit your dreams to what you think is possible, write down those things that you think are impossible and then make it a goal to achieve those very things.

Make Them Possible!

<u>First Question</u>:

WHAT DO YOU WANT TO BE IN LIFE?

Doctor, lawyer, Political Figure, Entrepreneur…

(For notes, use the Note Section at the end of each chapter.)

If you want to pursue more than one dream, I suggest you strategically create a plan that would lead you to that success. But for now, think of that one thing you like to do that you enjoy the most.

Ok, you got it? Now align your plans and life journey with that one thing that you enjoy doing the most. Then if you want to incorporate your other interests, create as many connecting pathways as you want along that same journey roadmap.

Example - When I was younger, I aspired to become a Soldier, but I also loved to dance. I wanted to become a Soldier and Dancer. Consequently, I chose the Army as my career path ("What I enjoyed the most") and Zumba Dancing as my hobby ("My other interest") until I was able to save enough money from

Zumba to pursue Fitness Instructing as another sustaining career (the connecting "Pathway" I created). Now, I am a Soldier and a Fitness Instructor. ("Plan executed").

Second Question:

WHAT IS EVERYTHING YOU WANT TO ACCOMPLISH/OR ACQUIRE IN LIFE?

Win Awards, Buy a House, Car, Spouse, Kids, Travel, Become a Role Model, Etc.

This question can have unlimited answers but focus on the major accomplishments you would like to achieve in life first. As you answer the question think about, HOW WILL YOU BETTER YOUR LIFE AND THE LIVES OF THOSE AROUND YOU? *Working hard and/or being a positive role model?* HOW WILL YOU MAKE A DIFFERENCE IN SOCIETY? Give back to the youth, become a volunteer, a mentor or a philanthropist?

Third Question:

WHAT STEPS DO YOU NEED TO TAKE TO ACHIEVE YOUR GOALS?

The steps you need to achieve your goals and dreams require (4) things:

1. Research

2. Asking Questions

3. Planning

4. Decision Making

Research. After you decide what you

want to be in life, you have to be proactive and research what it takes to become that which you choose. In doing your research (i.e. online or library), you can find out the best schools for your field, top employers hiring for that field, and the amount of money you can make in your field of choice. After you have done your research, you will then understand what it will take to become whatever you have decided to become and if it fits the vision of what you want to achieve.

Ask Questions. If you decide that you are still interested in that career at that point, find someone in that field that you look up to and ask them a few questions regarding that profession. Get some insight on the pros and cons with choosing that career choice.

Note: Only ask people who are knowledgeable about the career choice you are choosing because you never want to take advice from individuals who are not informed on the subject.

Plan. Start to look deep into how you are going to get from where you are, to where you want to be in life. Every plan that I have ever created started from within. I would sit in a quiet room, analyze my current situation and ask myself questions.

For Example, (Roadmap):

How will I become a Soldier,

- Graduate High school (w/good grades)

- Join ROTC to help pay for college

- Go to West Point

- Get my first job as a Lieutenant of

  a company size unit.

- Learn and develop my skills

- Gain credibility and go through the

ranks of promotion from Lieutenant, to

Captain, to Colonel, until I become a

Division Commander.

In order to achieve anything in life you have

to visualize it in your mind first and get a

clear view of exactly what you want.

Decision Making. Once you decide that you have seen enough and you feel confident that you can accomplish your dreams by putting in the necessary work, draw a roadmap (or vision board) of plans from start to finish. This plan should illustrate how you will get from where you are now to where you want to be in the future. Once your decisions are made and you are all in - Stick To The Plan!

Short Story

At the age of 18, I started noticing that I was mentally outgrowing my environment. You have to understand that where you are, doesn't define where you are going. Your past or present doesn't define your future. I remember that realization like it was yesterday, I was in my senior year of H.S and I had just gotten transferred to a new school.

As the new student I was very quiet but that allowed me to pay attention to what was really going on around me. I starting noticing that our teachers weren't teaching us anymore they were merely babysitting us. Students were focused on partying more than studying and here I was yearning to see the world. I wanted to see Europe, Africa, Asia and try all their different cuisines. This was a crucial moment where I not only had to make a key decision but I had to figure out how I was going to travel the world even though it seemed I had no way out of my environment.

It clicked to me that I loved JROTC, so joining the military may not only be fun, but also allow me the opportunity to travel the world. Once I realized I could make my dreams a reality I begin to focus more on where I wanted to go in life and I didn't hold back. I believed in myself more than anyone and made the decision to follow my dreams.

There will be key moments in your life where you have to make life changing decisions! Don't be scared to step out on faith. – Diamond McNulty

NOTES

CHAPTER 2 REVIEW

1. What are the (3) questions you should ask yourself when thinking about life?

2. What are the 4-steps you need to take to achieve your goals?

3. What is the name of the board you will create as your roadmap to success?

4. There will be _____ moments in your life where you have to make life-changing decision.

5. Never be afraid to step out on _____.

CHAPTER 3

Bestie, Ya Girls, and Associates

Surrounding Friendships

Friendship is very important on your journey toward success. Right now, you want to analyze your friends by asking them about their plans on becoming successful so that you can determine whether to keep those friends close or open your circle to finding new ones with similar values as you.

Friends come in different categories, for example:

(1) Entertainment Oriented Friends

- The Jokester

- The Relaxed and Amusing

(2) Business Oriented Friends

- Focused

- Crafty and/or Serious Natured

For instance, you have the Entertainment Oriented Friends who are great when it's time to party, relax and take your mind off work. But you don't want to get too distracted by the lack of focus some of these friends carry and lose sight of your plans and goals. Then you have the Business Oriented Friends, who are great when you are looking for personal development and ways to grow and improve toward success in life.

Each category of friends has their pros and cons. You might have some friends that you trust with your secrets, like to party and hang out with, but on a business level, they don't care to talk about future goals and plans. Not everyone will have goals and dreams, but no matter what you do, don't let anyone talk you out of yours. If you find yourself around dream killers, get rid of them. If you have friends that are well-rounded in both categories, that's great, but if not, your circle of friends should include a mixture of both Business Oriented and

Entertainment Oriented Friends in order to keep you focused and grounded.

Stay positive, stay focused and stay surrounded by motivated people who are headed in the same direction you are.

Don't Burn Bridges

What is burning bridges? Burning bridges refers permanently destroying a good relationships you once had, whether a business relationships or personal relationships that ended on a bad note. By burning that bridge, you are likely getting rid of a good relationship that you may need in the future. You may try to fix the relationship, but more than likely there is little you can do to get it back to the way it was once the damage has been done.

Allowing your attitude/temper to get the best of you by making senseless decisions could damage other ventures (goals) in life that you are trying to pursue.

Everyone you have had a bad encounter with could have a negative opinion of you when speaking to others. This could reflect badly when it comes to others helping you in the future, so maintain positive relationships. Remember, word of mouth is the most powerful way of marketing, whether it's through people or products. Learning to deal with negative situations in a positive way gives you the advantage.

When being faced with negativity, remember to stay calm and pay attention because there is always something to learn. You may need to distance yourself from someone or from a place where things are not going well. Basically, you want to get out of the situation without leaving a bad image of yourself (always try to be the bigger person).

Sometimes people will burn bridges with you, and you will have to make a decision whether they are worthy of having another chance at a relationship with you. Try to distance yourself from any drama and remember the word <u>value</u>. Is this relationship of any value to you? Think about it, can you benefit from having a relationship with this person? How much do you value this relationship? How much do they value you?

Your Future Circle

Your circle will change as you grow older and progress in life. This circle may consist of a few key people: your spouse, your circles of trustees (which are all the friends over the years you can look up to for guidance and call for answers), a banker, a lawyer, an accountant and other people who can assist in helping you grow personally, i.e. mentors.

Not only are they able to help you, but you should be able to help them as well. Go to the book store and grab a couple of books and read about what their jobs entail because you have to know how to utilize these individuals to the greatest extent. Build your team!

It took me a long time to learn everyone in my circle. I invested a lot of time and money in helping others who didn't help them or me. It took me a long time to realize my true value, and to surround myself with people like me who focus on success. In order to get to the next level in life you have to trust yourself and others.

You have to be able to make tough decisions and let go of the people that will hold you back. Surround yourself with dreamers. Keep this in mind that some people are assets and others are liabilities. Learning the true definition of assets and liabilities will make you more aware of what's really important, not only with people but in life.

Short Story

I wasn't very popular in middle school and like most teenage girls I longed for popularity and friendship. There was this group of blood sisters and brothers at Kenilworth Middle School that were popular, but for the wrong reasons. We will call them the Johnsons.

Getting into this group and being their friend was my ticket to popularity. The two oldest sisters told me that I had to start a fight in order to be a part of the group. The first fight I started was with a student who I knew was weaker than me. I walked into the math class and slapped her. I got suspended. I still was not fully apart of The Johnson's crew. I went to a few of their sleepovers and started to hang out with them.

One of the Johnson's told me another student was talking about me and when I get to social studies I had to fight her. I viciously attacked another student so badly that I was expelled from the school grounds. I had to go to an alternative school with former Marine Drill Sergeants and I never heard from the Johnson's again.

Moral of the Story: *The woman who follows the crowd will usually go no further than the crowd. The woman who walks alone is likely to find herself in places no one has ever been before.* – Albert Einstein

<u>NOTES</u>

CHAPTER 3 REVIEW

1. Name the two type of friends you will

have in life?

2. Define Burning Bridges?

3. Define Assets (Use Dictionary)?

4. Define Liabilities (Use Dictionary)?

CHAPTER 4

Make The Choice

Destroy Bad Habits

When it comes to having a habit I want you
to remember three things....

Habits Cost! Habits Cost! Habits Cost!

Not only do habits cost,
but bad habits like
smoking or excessive
drinking and drugs can
lead to major health problems. I never was a
smoker because if I added up the amount that
people would spend on cigarettes or other
smoking items, (i.e. weed) it is a ridiculous

amount of money. Now, if you can take all that money and put it in the bank or invest it into a business, you will benefit more.

Have fun in life but whatever you decide to do remember there are always consequences for your actions. Some people love to eat, some people love to party, some people love to travel or go to concerts... limit yourself according to your lifestyle (income vs. expenses).

Stay Out Of Trouble

Staying out of trouble is not hard to do unless you spend all your free time doing nothing. Fill all of your empty time with projects, whether you're cleaning the house, organizing your ideas, reading a book, or anything that's productive.

Remember one wrong decision can be life changing and may cause you to be sent to jail or cost you your life. Surround yourself with positive people from the beginning and let everything negative fade off.

Wait To Have Kids

In today's society, more kids are having kids. I can honestly say it's hard for me, at the age of 24, living on my own, taking care of bills, budgeting and balancing the everyday situations that occur to even consider a baby. I can only imagine all the things I would have to sacrifice in order to take care of a child.

Take your time, and don't have kids until you get married. If you can manage to beat the odds, you will thank me because feelings change as you grow and people change as they grow. You don't want to jeopardize your future by being reckless and possibly becoming dependent on your parents to raise you and your children. Life is about balance, making smart decisions and protecting yourself.

There are <u>5</u> reasons why I would suggest you not having any kids at an early age:

1. Live Out Your Youth

2. Finish School – Build A Career

3. Travel

4. Find The Right Person

5. Build Your Finances

Live Out Your Youth. As a child, you don't have many responsibilities and you depend on your parents or guardians for much of your protection whether it's food, shelter or clothing. As you get older and more mature, you will start to make better decisions and support yourself and your own children if need be. By having children at a young age, you could slow your own development and stagger your mental growth due to the sudden responsibilities of parenthood. Never limit yourself, your lifestyle or a child's lifestyle due to bad decisions.

Finish School – Build A Career. Finishing school and starting a career before you have children is great. Not only will you have more time on your hands, you will be in a position to support your family financially, because you are finished with school and into your career earning a living.

Travel. How many vacations have you been on so far? You can travel the world before and after you have kids. If you travel before kids, not only will it be cheaper but you will have the freedom to explore and party without having to worry about having kids to take care of. Once you have kids, it might be hard to find a baby sitter in order for you to go out and party. The added responsibility is definitely a life changer.

Find The Right Person. As you get older you will develop into a different individual. You will gain more values in life and you will outgrow some people. It is best to wait until you develop into the person you will become and wait to meet a significant other who has developed as well. Give yourself time to develop, see the world and meet the right person before you have kids. No regrets.

Finances. Do you have enough money to support yourself? Can you pay your own bills? Can you buy your own clothes and food? After you finish school, establish a career, travel a bit, find the right person and marry them, then you will be able to sit down together and financially say you are ready to start a family. Kids cost money and require time. Build your bank account, buy a house, and get yourself financially set for a child before you have one.

By financially, I mean make sure you can afford a child and everything thing that comes with having one. Clothes, food, pampers, shelter, daycare, and schooling.

I want you to talk with your parents or guardians and get their input on bearing kids as well. <u>Set yourself up for success!</u> As I said earlier, it is hard for me at 24, working, paying bills and going to school. I could only imagine how it would be with a child to take care of.

Short Story

By my junior year of high school, I had the realization that if I wanted to stay out of trouble I had to keep busy. At that point I had already been expelled twice from school so what I decided to do was become more active after school. I was already on the drill team, but that was only twice a week. I then decided to join the dance team, but that was only twice a week, so I decided to join the science and math club, which was one day a week.

After a few months of being a part of all of these activities I started to get recognized for my service to the school for being captain of the drill team, the choreographer for the dance team, a member of the science and math club, and a member of the color guard. I received multiple recognitions but what I realized within myself was, I stop getting in trouble. Later on in life JROTC helped me with my military career and being a part of the dance team helped me with my fitness-instructing career.

Moral of the Story: Fill your time with extracurricular activities and staying out of trouble will become second nature.

NOTES

CHAPTER 4 REVIEW

1. Fill in the Blank. Habits_____!

2. Name one way that you can stay out of trouble?

3. You should wait to have kids until you are?

4. Name (5) reasons you shouldn't have kids at an early age?

1. _____

2. _____

3. _____

4. _____

5. _____

CHAPTER 5

A Woman's Worth

Gaining Respect

Respect is hard to gain and easy to lose. Once you master how to gain respect, the closer you will get to becoming successful.

You gain respect in several different ways:

- Working Hard

- Show Respect to Others

- Show Persistence

- Walk the Walk

In order to gain respect in life, you have

to be a person who shows leadership qualities and possess great character. People respect those who want things out of life, work hard, possess knowledge, and those who can have a conversation about living their dreams. No one respects people who joke around all day, sit around doing nothing and tell lies. Even though the truth sometimes hurts, you will always be respected for telling the truth.

I'm not saying not to joke around sometimes but first make sure you have everything in order to go along with those jokes.

Work Hard. Beat people at their own

game! If you are at work and your boss wants you to work hard, work harder. You gain more respect by exceeding people expectations.

Show Respect to Others. Be genuine, but stand up for what you believe and be smart enough to get down and dirty for your respect. However, try to distance yourself from situations where it may lead to you throwing others under the bus. Everyone deserves to be respected. Try to avoid confrontation by walking away from hostile and disrespectful people, and environments that might escalate into unnecessary actions.

Show Persistence. Whether you know it or not everyone around you is watching your work ethic and how you carry yourself. Are you a person who quits easy or are you a fighter? Do you get the job done and go for more? Why do you want to be successful? Use your reason as motivation to never give up and you will gain a lot of respect especially by keeping a positive attitude.

Walk the Walk. Means "practice what you preach" at all times. If you say something is wrong, then do not do what you said is wrong. Do what you say and say what you mean! Keep your promises, and if you know you might not be able to keep them, don't make the promise.

Respecting Yourself

Respecting yourself is crucial especially in today's society if you expect others to respect you. Being able to take life seriously and knowing every step you take can potentially be a step forward to success or a step away from it.

- This could be as simple as not being a class clown.

- This could be as simple as choosing a beautiful knee length skirt over a mini skirt.

- This could be ignoring a very attractive male yelling, *"Aye Yo Ma, let me get ya number."*

Since you respect yourself enough you won't respond. You deserve to be approached, as a young lady should, in the highest regard. No one will respect you unless you respect yourself.

> **Virtuous:** Having or showing high moral standards.

Men appreciate and respect virtuous

women. This is why while you are young, you must focus on school and becoming the best person you can be.

Respectable young men appreciate a woman of class and women of class carry themselves with the most upright dignity, sound judgment, and sophistication.

Core Values. When getting to know someone you should start by paying attention to their values. Values are what they believe in. It is important to pay close attention to the people that you are around and be able to understand their value system. Not only is this system important for significant other, but it is also important for friends and family members as well.

Knowing what a persons values are will show you whether you can relate to them or not. **Here are a few great values to look for in someone:** Dependability, Honesty, Motivational, Inspirational, Respectful, and Loyalty. Being Fun, Loving, Passionate, Educated and Positive are also great values to look for as well.

Be Yourself. Who Are You? Looking back at some of the values above, start to ask yourself questions that can show who you are. Are you funny or not? … Don't Lie ☺ !

After you determine your own personal values write down <u>5</u> below.

Personal Value List:

1.

2.

3.

4.

5.

Hint #1

Look out for people who only want to be around you because of what you have instead of whom you are. They are not worth your time. They are referred to as opportunists.

Hint #2

Never use your charm and abilities for selfish pleasures. Stay positive! Find a significant other who you could see yourself building something with such as a family and a career. You must think about if they are mentally strong enough to be your spouse!

Hint #3

People love talking about the future especially with an ambitious young woman with dreams.

Relationships. As you get older you will start looking for a significant other. How do you know if they are worthy?

- Pay attention.

- Feel the vibe.

- Never lie to yourself.

   Example: If you were dating a young man watch how he handles himself when other girls try to talk to him. It is not your job to say anything unless she disrespects him after he turns her down. Try to let him handle himself, that way you don't have to get into any serious altercations.

   You are becoming a woman and the way you carry yourself will show if you're classy or not. However, if he giggles and flirts then you know he's not ready for you. He has to be firm and serious about the bond between the two of you.

Equality is important too; your significant other should do for you just as you do for them because this is a relationship.

Example - You buy them a birthday gift and they should buy you a birthday gift as well. Sometimes you may want to switch things up and take them out – and that's ok. You both should give and receive in order to feel appreciated.

Communication is the biggest thing when it comes to developing any relationship. You both have to communicate about everything—even things that aren't comfortable to talk about. You will feel more comfortable once things are out in the open. Your personal business is your business. Keep your relationship information between you and your partner because there are people who just may want to steal one of you or break you up.

Becoming the kind of woman who communicates has it's advantages because even though you are in control, you don't have to brag and boast because your significant other already knows who you are. They know you are a young, smart, hardworking, talented young woman and they do not want to lose you. So relax because if they are smart they won't mess things up. If you chose the right person you will feel the same way. This way, you both will appreciate the <u>value</u> of each other.

Make every effort to make things happen as planned. You have to be the ultimate woman. Not too cocky, but confident... humble, but not a pushover... loving, but stern! Live everyday "One Day at a Time." Plan for tomorrow but focus on the daily tasks at hand.

Respect All People

Based on my own life learned statics...

- Being negative and disrespectful cuts off 50% of the chances for you to succeed

- Being racist cuts off another 25%

It is best that you love all, work hard, and stay positive in order to be a force in this society! True leaders understand that we live in a systematic world and there is a certain cycle of good and evil no matter what race you are. If you are black or white, rich or poor, you have an opportunity to be the best you can be throughout your lifetime.

Depending on where you start, you might have to work harder than others. While you are working hard and others are relaxing remember that you are gaining on them in this race to become successful.

Short Story

Being in a male dominated career field, I must be able to hold my own and keep up with my male counter-parts. This being said, I never carry my <u>assertive</u> attitude from work into my home. I am happily married and always carry myself in ways my husband would be proud to scream to the world that I am his wife.

My husband and I leave for work at 7a.m. and normally return home around 7pm. I make sure to go immediately to the kitchen and prepare dinner. While making sure the laundry is done, and the house is clean. As a result my husband always pulls out my chair, open doors for me, take me out to dinner when I am too tired to cook, etc.

We have a mutual understanding of our roles and we respect what each other bring to the table. I would never try to talk over my husband while in public, but I never have to because he always asks for my opinion. He respects me because I am a powerful woman that takes pride in letting my husband lead our household.

When you respect everyone they will respect you back. Becoming a person of respect starts at the beginning when you first meet an individual and throughout your time knowing that person. You have to stay on point at all times. Respect is hard to gain and easy to lose. – Diamond McNulty

NOTES

CHAPTER 5 REVIEW

1. Fill in the blank. Respect is hard to gain

and _____ .

2. Name (3) ways you gain respect?

3. Name (2) things you need to be or have in

order to be successful around women?

4. You can tell a lot about a woman by her

core _____ .

5. Being negative and disrespectful cuts off

_____% chances for you to succeed.

6. Being racist cuts off _____% chances

for you to succeed.

CHAPTER 6

Fundamentals To Know & Practice

Reading

Have you ever heard the saying that if you want to hide something from someone, to put it in a book? Well the saying is true! Personally, in high school I loved to read. Books were an escape from the life I was living and I learned early that EVERYTHING in life is linked to reading.

Imagine you are a CEO of your own company. One of your workers created a proposal to add something new or fresh to improve the company that will allow you to make billions. But, you were not able to comprehend what you were reading. That would be a disaster. Reading is like watering all of the dream seeds inside of you. If you want your dreams to grow you will need to water them.

Whenever my brother Diamond wants to learn something, he buys a book on it. He self educates on everything in his free time through reading and has built multiple companies on his own from reading books. Reading skills are non-negotiable on your journey to becoming successful.

Reading and buying books on your own can save you a lot of time and money. It also allows you to meet great people, share knowledge or exchange books and gain personal information that the average person may not know or utilize.

It is critical to remember that knowledge is the key that will open doors! We live in a world that swallows the weak. One negative court case and you're cursed for life, depending on your environment. The only way to beat the odds is to stay out of trouble, educate yourself and create your own worth. If you happen to get in trouble and it leads to you being convicted of a crime, it will be a challenge to get a good job.

Therefore, having knowledge will allow you to start your own business. If necessary, and you think like me, who really wants to work for someone else his or her whole life anyway?

Self-motivation and Persistence

Self-motivation is the force that drives you to action.

Persistence is continuing to do a task in spite of how difficult it is or the opposition you face.

Self-motivation and persistence is something you must have on your journey to success because not everyone will support you or tell you that you are doing a good job. With that being said, don't dwell on the thoughts of others or past failures.

Reflecting on the past is ok but it is better to focus on today in order to better your tomorrow! If you got bad grades last quarter, don't dwell on them. Start studying so you can get better grades next time.

Challenge yourself, I know I am cramming a lot of important information in your head and you are probably being filled with the excitement to read more. I honestly want you to open your mind and take everything I'm saying into account, so that it sticks with you for the rest of your life. Keep referring to this book so you can become successful and stay successful.

Faith and Motivation

Faith and Motivation play a big part on your road to becoming successful. Success is based on how your mind processes the events in your life. Think...your brain is a tool so use it to its full potential. When you are stuck in certain situations, Think! The situation is not permanent, it is temporary and it will be over soon.

You will value every lesson you get from going through it. Also, the more mistakes you make the greater your chances are of becoming successful. Typically, it's best to learn from other people mistakes which is why I stress listening to older individuals who can give you insight to save you from going through the same things they did.

Believe that all things are possible. Stick to your beliefs with the ultimate sacrifice to yourself, that you can do anything. I, Diamond McNulty remember when I was at my lowest point in life in 2008, instead of letting negativity get the best of me; I used that lowest point as my motivation.

At that moment, since I was at the bottom of the bottom the only place for me to go was to the top. I sat in my car and laughed because it was funny. All the lessons I was learning at that moment, from who was really by my side, to what got me to that point, to thinking this will never happen again.

In order to truly become successful, you have to overcome many obstacles—this will make you a stronger individual. This world is not for the weak. But there are benefits for those people who go through the darkness to see the sunny days—trust me they are worth every moment.

Use your family as support and your obstacles as motivation to never stop. Stay focused on the target. A lot of people won't believe in your dreams like you believe, but that's the defining moment of your faith—something that you can't see or grasp but you still choose to believe.

Short Story

Three months before I, Diamond left Chicago I was sleeping in my car after my family was split up. I decided to move into my grandmothers five-bedroom house on the

Southside of Chicago to bounce back. My uncle immediately kicked me out of my grandmother's house and told me I couldn't stay there. There was only one other person living there at the time, I was hurt beyond belief that he would rather push me to the street instead of letting me live there.

I remember sitting in my car laughing because that was the lowest point I had ever been in my life. I was so faith driven that I asked God to show me everything I needed to see at that moment.

At that moment I learned who was truly my friends, who had my back and I said I will never get that low ever again. I slept at my girlfriends house a few days but her mother didn't really want me there and I respected that. I called (my father figure) who had been in my life since I was two years old and he told me to bring everything I had to his house and I could sleep on his couch.

That meant a lot to me especially since my mother at that time didn't know I was out on the streets. I could have called my mother and slept on her couch but she had a one-bedroom apartment and I didn't want to run to her, I decided to stand strong on my own.

Skipping forward to when I moved to Atlanta from Louisiana I ran out of money and I called my mother who had just found out that I was homeless before from my ex-girlfriend in Chicago, and she was heartbroken. I told her about my situation with my rent and she cleared her savings account to pay my rent. I was so upset because I was almost homeless again and I felt like a failure. Here I was still taking risk after risk but deep down inside me I knew I was becoming a success story. After she paid my rent I got a call from a job one week later and started working at a hotel in Atlanta.

If I would have given up I probably would have ran back home and never fulfilled my destiny. When times get hard it's easy to give up and it's hard to hold on. After that moment I made it a habit to do everything that was hard in life as a challenge to myself, to see if I could overcome it.

Sometimes you will fall but you have to dust yourself off and keep going. You will have family members that will hurt you but you have to keep going. Every time I hit rock bottom I told myself I would be the richest man in America and I kept pushing towards my goal. - Diamond McNulty

<u>NOTES</u>

CHAPTER 6 REVIEW

1. Finish the quote: "If you want to hide

something from someone put it in

_____."

2. "Knowledge is the _____ that will

open doors."

3. "Reading books can save

you_____ and _____."

Define Self- Motivation?

Define Persistence?

Define Faith?

CHAPTER 7

A Woman's Strength

"A woman's heart should be so hidden in God that a man has to seek him just to find her.

– Maya Angelou

Superwoman

You are powerful and valuable. However, it's up to you to utilize your power and appreciate your value.

Natural Power. The older you get you begin to tap into the natural powers that you were born with. You are the cement of the family that solidifies the foundation and men are the foundation. As you grow you will realize that

112

it is through you that life is created, nurtured and developed. Women are a *Secret Jewel*. Since you are a jewel the first thing you have to figure out is…

How much are you worth?

Let's take a moment to answer this… **You Are Priceless.**

Understanding that you are priceless adds unlimited value to you. Don't give your power or attention away to just anyone.

Abusing your power. Abusing anything is not good especially the power you are born with. Being born with this woman power does not mean you can get a free ride through life. Women can dress up, put on make-up, throw on some hair and have guys drooling over her. She could make a living using people.

This is when most women realize the power within them, but the moment you fall into that lifestyle... you lose that power IMMEDIATELY! The power is decreasing every time you abuse it. Each person you use and abuse takes away pieces of your power. **Women are most powerful when they realize what they are capable of and choose to use that power to drive them.** Drive them to become CEOs, Military

Generals, A-list Actresses, Doctors and Lawyers.

So the decision is yours, will you give your powers away for quick happiness or hold on to it and let it drive you to make you better? Live the lifestyle only some can dream of, courtesy of your own hard work.

Confidence vs. Cocky

Confidence: *A state of being certain.*

Cocky: *Conceited or arrogant.*

Like I mentioned in Chapter 1 your success depends on your confidence in you. Confidence comes from looking at and inside yourself and believing that you are mentally and physically brilliant. However, confidence has an evil twin called cocky which can become a bad thing for some successful people who like to gloat. When you start to achieve success you must learn to stay grounded as you grow.

Staying grounded as you grow will show that you have good character and will allow you to succeed even higher because those around you will appreciate your sportsmanship and cheer you on. Being cocky can cause you to lose friends and make people wish for your downfall because no one likes to feel stepped on by anyone, so if you do succeed try not to crush others on the way up. There is a saying that the same people you see on the way up, you will have to see on your way down. Be respectful.

The New Woman

Did you know you're a part of a great time in history for women? We as women have evolved so quickly and so gracefully. Just 100 years ago we were only wearing dresses, discouraged from pursuing higher education and not allowed to vote. Furthermore we only worked at home, in small department stores and men were allowed to beat us.

We have always been considered the weaker gender, not able to think and create on our own. It took the world to go into wars and our men to be deployed for society to begin to realize how much more we could achieve. While the men fought the wars we kept cities running, by leaving home and doing the jobs our men would normally do.

In 1920, we earned our right to vote and as of 2016 we have a front runner female Presidential Candidate. We are CEOs, Military Leaders, Entrepreneurs, Supreme Court Judges, Astronauts and Politicians. There is nothing stopping us, nothing standing in our way and we can blaze any trial offered on this green earth. Our power and influence is endless.

Short Story

I, Mercedes shipped off to basic training and when I got there, no one carried my heavy bags, everyone carried their own bags. No one cared I had to do my hair, everyone had the same exact time to get dressed and be outside in formation.

No one cared I felt mud was icky, when one of us in the platoon messed up we all had to roll (exercise) in mud. No one cared that my ruck sack (book bag) was heavy, we all had to carry 35lbs. No one cared that due to pedicures my feet were delicate, we all had to ruck 12 miles. Now that I'm out of basic training and a leader in the Military, I have the same concept. I expect my female Soldiers to complete their battle drills, investigations, classes, or instructions just as the male Soldiers. I do not treat neither gender special or different. Since we are trained that both male and female must always adhere to Military standards.

The career I chose and most careers in this day and age can care less if you are a woman. Why? Because we have evolved and proven to be just as good in most occupations as our male counter parts. Keep this with you, work your hardest and continue to evolve our gender through being the best at whatever you are doing.

Your destiny is determined by how many times you try again. There is no giving up! There is no " I quit"! If you have to cry then cry and get back to work. Success is very painful which is why only the strong survive it. – Diamond McNulty

<u>NOTES</u>

CHAPTER 7 REVIEW

1. You are powerful and _____.

2. How much are you worth?

    _____.

3. In 1920 we earned our right to

    _____.

4. Women are the cement of the family and

men are the _____.

Chapter 8

Start The Journey To Success

Develop Leadership

Between the ages of 7-13 I was responsible for watching over my siblings after school while my mother worked. Being one of the oldest I had to make sure the house was clean, homework was done, make sure all uniforms were taken off, dinner was eaten, baths were taken, and everyone was in bed at their bed time before mom came home. Even when my little brother was born I had additional responsibilities until all my siblings were old enough to take care of themselves. If it wasn't done I got in trouble in which some of the punishment included not being able to watch TV or being able to go outside. As I got older I learned to appreciate my upbringing because in my current leadership role I take full responsibility for my Soldiers actions while my leadership reprimands me for my Soldiers wrong doing. I now understand that because I am responsible for them it's my job to make sure their duties get done.

Are you a leader or a follower?

A leader is someone who people look up to.

A leader is someone who takes

responsibility.

A leader is someone who creates a vision.

A leader is someone who encourages.

A leader can communicate clearly.

A leader is confident and inspirational.

A leader is dedicated and creative.

A leader has a positive attitude.

Leaders Lead

To practice good leadership skills, it starts at home with your family. Whether you are the oldest child or the youngest in the family, it is your duty to help lead the family. Your siblings should look to you for protection and see that you can deliver. With your focus and positive attitude, within a short time it will be hard for others not to want to be around you.

Be the one influencing others to travel down the right path instead of letting them influence you to go down the wrong path. <u>Be A Leader!</u> Remember, a follower travels behind someone to imitate his or her movements or ideas.

Again, Stay out of Trouble

How to stay out of trouble? Choose your friends wisely and don't ditch classes. We've covered the types of friends you should have in your circle, but we didn't discuss the types of friends you should not have in your circle. Some young men and women around you are into negative things that you should not be involved with.

Peer pressure (influence from others) is big with young women who do not know how to say, **NO.** You have a strong-mind right? So you should not have a problem saying **NO** to the pressure of drugs, alcohol, or any other reckless activity. Remember, you are in control of what you do. No one can ever make you do anything you don't want to do. You Are Smart - Make Smart Decisions. **Be A Leader Not A Follower!**

Education & Financial Literacy

Financial Literacy (the ability to understand
how money works in the world).

Money is to make more money!

Take a moment, look at the chart and picture below:

Education Level	Potential Status	Potential Lifestyle	Potential Influence	Potential Earnings of Money (Yearly)
Entrepreneur	Outer Space	Unlimited	High	Unlimited
Grad School	Moon	High	High	100,000+
College	Sky	Med-High	Med-High	60,000+
High school	Tree	Medium	Medium	+/_ 40,000
Grammar School	Ground	Minimum	Minimum	+/_ 25,000

© 2014 Empire Imagery. All Rights Reserved.

The picture above describes the levels in life when it pertains to the different levels of education. The higher the level you reach the more money you can acquire. The biggest difference in this picture is that an entrepreneur stands at the top of everything.

Have you ever heard the greater the risk the greater the reward? To become an entrepreneur, you can acquire any level of education, but you standout by taking the risk of starting your own business. Some entrepreneurs fail and some succeed. However, if you don't take the risk you will never achieve the rewards to go with it.

Traditional education is very important in developing your personal growth but if you want to become an entrepreneur you will have to work twice as hard and become a leader in business.

Advice: Don't get rich and go broke! Financial literacy is very important when becoming successful. What is money? How to use money? How not to use money? How do you make the most out of each dollar? If you are paid allowance as a child, it is very important that you use your money wisely because this is the beginning stage to managing money. Money should be used to make more money! Every time you get money, you should think about how it could be used to make more money.

College does not guarantee success or guarantee that you will make a lot of money. However, there are special benefits that come with higher education. We will teach you skills that you can use in life to become successful.

Don't be too hard on yourself if you get a B instead of an A on a test. Challenge yourself and do better next time. Use your shortcomings as motivation to do better. Just continue to be your best at everything you do.

Don't let anyone try to make you believe that you cannot achieve something—because anything is possible. Learn how to tell yourself that you did a good job because it builds strength.

"Do your best and forget the rest".

– Tony Horton

Learn To Network

As you start to travel, you will learn a lot about people, their lifestyles and their culture. After meeting someone you should be able to tell right away if they are someone who can help you or hinder you by the way they communicate.

If they are goal-oriented and business-minded, you should invite them into your circle and carefully get to know them better. If they are not positive, don't waste your time because people can distract you from what's really important in life. Every day is a great day to show the world how focused you are and you don't have to be arrogant or big-headed about it. You've got what it takes to be great—just continue to be humble but focused and you will go further than you've ever imagined.

Networking with people is part of the building process of your empire and plan. When you tell people your dreams, they might look at you like you're crazy, but remember to **BE BOLD**. Your actions speak louder than words, so continue to show and prove.

You will meet people everywhere you go from school, work, church, and even from different parts of the world. The world is one big network and the more access you have, the more beneficial it can become to you. There is a saying that "Your Network defines your Net Worth". Meaning the people, you are surrounded by create your value. Just by who you know you might be able to get discounts on certain things, get into places you never knew existed and be invited into different circles. Take advantage of every opportunity.

Short Story

I, Mercedes won every single Best Warrior Competition I competed in for the first four years in the Military. However, the last two years I have placed second. When you know you are a winner it is hard to accept losing, especially while being a leader. So to get some advice, I reached out to my brother Diamond who told me a story that motivated me to never give up.

Here's the story...

"Ever since I was 6 years old my baseball team won 2nd place. I came in second place so many times I got numb to losing and I learned how to become a true champion. Many times people who win 1st place early in life feel so accomplished that they don't strive for anything else in life.

My senior year in High School we made it to the championship game one last time. At this point in my life I had already won a cooking scholarship for $24,000 for college and this would be my last game as a baseball player.

We were down by 6 runs in the last inning. I was up to bat with bases loaded, 2 outs, 2 strikes on me and my heart was pumping. My whole team was yelling Diamante... Diamante. I took a step back from the plate to breath! My final thought was "It's Not Over Until We Win". I hit a shot to right field that was dropped by the right fielder and we rallied to win the championship game. That was one of the greatest moments of my life! At our Awards ceremony I was awarded MVP for leading our team to victory."

This story kept me motivated and reminded me that even though you feel you are a first place winner, it's okay to come in second but never give up, one day you will be back in first.

Sometimes you need a refresher, which is why you surround yourself with great people.

No matter how many times you come in second place your greatest victory is yet to come. Instead of rolling over and giving up I chose to fight and focus because my team needed me to deliver. In the time of desperation your team will need you, your family will need you and your future children will need you to step up to the plate and bring it home. It's always easy for us to put the game in someone else's hands, but when you take control of your life, your future and walk in your purpose, you will become successful. – Diamond McNulty

NOTES

CHAPTER 8 REVIEW

1. Name two characteristics of leadership?

2. To practice good leadership skills, start at

_____.

3. How do you stay out of trouble?

4. When dealing with peer pressure its best to

say?

5. Define Financial Literacy?

6. Money is to make more_____.

7. Networking with people is part of your

_____ process.

8. Your _____ determines your Net

Worth.

CHAPTER 9

Easy As 1, 2, 3

Think Big

Do you want to be the player on the team or the owner of the team? Back-up dancer or own the studio with dancers assigned to you? A lot of kids play sports with hopes of becoming a professional athlete, or like me passionate about dancing. Since everyone can't make it in professional sports or dancing, you need to have a backup plan to fall back on while you are working towards your goals.

Have you ever heard anyone say "I want

to become the owner of a sports team?" Trust me if you think athletes make a lot of money imagine how much money the owners make in order to pay the players... A lot!

Create and Follow Your Goals

Creating Goals should be setup in (2) categories:

- Short Term Goals
- Long Term Goals

Short Term Goals are goals that you set from today up to the next 5 years.

Long Term Goals are goals that you set from the 5th year up to 10 years plus.

First things first, you will need a few things to get started:

- A blank notebook and a pencil (so you are able to erase and make changes if needed)

- Write down "NOW" at the top of the page (your "POINT A")

- Write down where you want to be at the bottom of the page (your "POINT B")

- Then depending on where you are in life, write down everything you need to get you from Point A to Point B (example - money, computers, knowledge (school), people you need to meet, etc.) in the specific order of attainment.

♦ Write down an estimate of how long it will take you to get through each step whether you need to save money, if you need to work a second job or join a networking organization. Although it might take a couple of years for you to go to school and save money: <u>Stick to the plan</u>! If you have a team of people and they all quit on you: <u>Stick to the plan</u>!

Growth. You might invest a lot of time

and money into your dreams and things might not go as planned. Be assured, going through all the pain and confusion will be worth it. You will learn what went wrong and why it went wrong. Don't make the same mistakes twice. Take your time and follow your faith so that you don't become like others and quit. It may take you 2 or 3 times or more to get it right!

Ask questions to older and trustworthy people; they have great advice.

In order to win, you have to set yourself up for success 100%. Do not buy anything without having at least twice the amount of money in your account. Spend a dollar save a dollar. Try to stay out of debt.

Learn about what you're getting yourself into before you jump head first into it. Remember:

(Books – Books – Books) Research!

No matter what happens, Never give up!

Stick to the Plan

Sticking to the plan is critical when it comes to becoming successful. Developing your plan is the first step! Throughout your next couple of years as you work towards your goals, you will encounter obstacles that will distract you from your main focus.

Throughout the pain, suffering, confusion, anxiety, helplessness, depressed days and nights you have to pick yourself up and stick to the plan. Strength is something that you have to acquire long before you start this journey.

Have the ability to do for self and live your life as if you're the only one—meaning, don't depend on anyone or anything. Asking for help is one thing but depending on someone is another. The more you depend on others the weaker you become. It's always great to have people in your corner who can help you but you want to have the mindset like those people are not really there...as if there is no safety net if you fail. Failure is not an option.

Short Story

I sat down for months and repeatedly met up with my laptop to create and reach out to you and all young women through written word. I wanted you to know that you are beautiful, nothing is standing in your way, and that I genuinely love and care about you. I'd go to my laptop and dream of a world where it is the NORM for a young woman to be a successful Entrepreneur, CEO, Military Leader, Scientist, or President of this country.

I thought of you with every word I typed hoping it would capture and inspire you. Why? Well as I typed from the heart I wanted you to realize you are worthy, amazing, strong, smart, and very capable of being anything in this world! I sat thinking of you accomplishing your goals and grabbing life by the horns. I imagined you providing business propositions in other languages. I imagined you being a VERY SUCCESSFUL YOUNG WOMAN.

Your destiny is determined by how many times you try again. There is no giving up! There is no " I quit"! If you have to cry then cry and get back to work. Success is very painful which is why only the strong survive it. – Diamond McNulty

NOTES

CHAPTER 9 REVIEW

1. You should always think_____ when planning your goals.

2. You should always have a backup_____ to fall back on when working towards your goals.

3. Define Short Term Goals?

4. Define Long Term Goals?

5. No matter what happens on your road to success you should Never_____.

6. _____is something that you have to acquire long before you start this journey.

CHAPTER 10

Becoming A Success

The Mind For Success

How do you prepare yourself for pain? The stronger you are, the less painful things are mentally and physically, so learn to laugh at it and get back to business. Don't consume yourself with the millions of problems in the world that can take you off your "A" Game. You only can do what you can do. Work harder than everyone and push it pass the limit.

I, Diamond worked three jobs around the clock 7 days straight for 6 months, I eventually cut it down to two so that I could free up time to complete another goal. I analyzed my plan, took time to think, and then moved to another city that was better suited to complete that plan. I went to film school and then again, got two jobs as I built multiple companies. I read business books and attended school on my off days. Don't let anything stop you. Make it happen. Work harder than everyone.

Organization plays a big role when you start to get to this level. When I left Chicago, my focus was on getting my family to a better place. My mind said I'm going to "Take over the world" and this is how I'm going to do it. Plan, Plan, Plan!

When you want something so bad it's hard to sleep. My motto is NO SLEEP, GOTTA GET IT... I rarely felt tired and after 5 years here we are!

When you are doing things that are outside the box and striving for greatness, the attitude of those around you will shift from looking at you like you're crazy, to having crazy respect for you; eventually placing you on a high pedestal.

Remember keep going and focus... don't gloat or get bigheaded. This is just the beginning. When I first started, I found myself working with people who were lazy and didn't want to put in the work it took to become successful. When this happens, it is best to cut them off and get back to business...just that simple.

There is no time to waste, when you are headed to the top... let's go! Nothing more to talk about...you are going to the top. Never limit yourself. Never say you can't do something, just do it.

One thing I have noticed about myself is

that I always fit better being around older people because we think on the same level. We all believe that life is not a game. My circle was and still is full of skilled individuals with different strengths who think like me.

If I meet you once, I already know if you are genuine. I pick up on things quickly and depending on our conversation the connection will be built or broken instantly. I'm a great Chef but I have no problem washing dishes, if that's what it takes to get where I am trying to go. You have to start somewhere.

What also keeps me motivated, is remembering how much my mother sacrificed for me. It's a goal of mine to become the best I can be. Not only because I'm working hard to take over the world, but also because I'm going to give her the opportunity to relax. She deserves it.

Don't be a burden to others, especially your parents just because they will do anything for you. Don't abuse them. Make their life easier. Everyone may not be a supporter but everyone means something. Have respect for all people.

You will become very successful but

along with success comes responsibility—
what is the plan after you become successful?
How many lives will you change? I have a
full-blown plan because all I do is think and
plan.

Most people don't use their brain to it's
full potential. <u>Use Yours</u>! Who cares if
someone else was born filthy rich and you
were born poor? Who cares that your father
wasn't there? Who cares what you didn't
have? I'll let you in on a little secret, the
world does not care! Your life is in your
hands.

Once you hit 18 and older, you are

responsible for yourself. Take the negative that has been thrown your way and turn it into a positive.

Are you willing to leave everything behind to chase your dream? Are you willing to sleep on the floor and barely eat? We all have to start somewhere. When others are working, I'm working. While others are watching TV, I'm working. When they are sleep, I'm just coming home, taking a shower, and planning the future while I shower. Brushing my teeth and building my team, laying down and planning for tomorrow. <u>Don't stop! Keep going.</u>

If you've been to one party you've been to them all. If you focus now, by the time you're older you will have accomplished your goals and have become a successful young woman.

I didn't know how to cook, write music, rap, create logos, create websites, film movies, or play chess until I studied those crafts and built those skills. Everyone doubted me except for a handful of people. My mind was made up from the beginning that I had a few talents and I wanted to get better at them all.

If cooking didn't work, I would do film. If

film didn't work, I would do music. I worked them all at the same time so that no matter what happened I would be successful. I would cook and create songs while at work, visually planning the videos, and creating the website concept all at once in my head.

Many people focus on one thing at a time, but I have a different belief system. When I was 16, my mentor Mr. Muhammad told me to never put all my eggs in one basket. I stuck to that belief and it has gotten me far in life.

Every business minded individual should learn business and accounting. You have to study hard in order to master your future. Adopt a mind for success. Anything is possible!

THE SECRET TO SUCCESS

The Law of Attraction is the secret to success. Meaning – surround yourself with things and people that will keep you in line with your goals. Also, you have to speak success into existence! The more you say things and act on them, the more likely you will achieve them. People follow people who they can trust because; Great Leaders Lead.

That secret is already out, but applying that secret is the key to success. Knowing and applying are two different things. Everyday I open my eyes with a positive attitude and tell myself, "I'm going to take over the world." I have "<u>Faith</u>" which means I believe that my dreams and visions will come true, given the hard work and dedication I put towards making them happen. When anyone would ask me how I was doing I would say "I'm doing great, taking over the world one day at a time." Everyday those were my words! And I truly applied that to my life.

In my living room, I put a map up of the world so that every time I'm on my computer

I can see it. Whenever I take a trip or travel to a place or even meet someone from another state or country I mark it on my map! I started asking different people from different countries what kind of businesses they had in their country, and what they wanted to really do outside of their current jobs because some people also have dreams that might align with yours. I dream of bettering the world and helping someone else.

I hope you have received all of this information and that you take it to heart. You should have great intentions and now you should feel more equipped to accomplish your goals in life. We wish you much success, love and happiness on Becoming A Successful Young Woman.

Short Story

The older I get the more thankful I am. You can gain a lot by being a good person. Two of the most important things that helped me become successful were, taking advantage of every program that was available to me to help expand my talents/skills, and having great mentors who guided me on my path to success.

At 7 years old my mother placed me in the Chicago Youth Programs, in which every Saturday they took us on field trips and paired us up with professional mentors who not only tutored us but also cared about us. I am very grateful to Dr. Joe DiCara and Dr. Karen Sheehan because that one seed that was planted 20 years ago will change the lives of children around the world. Thank you to the full CYP staff, mentors, Josephine and Bill Johnson.

You see giving is a domino effect and we all must do our job to pay it forward as well. I am very active when it comes to teaching kids how to live their dreams and when that child becomes successful it is their responsibility to pay it forward as well.

Every summer my mother allowed me to play on the baseball team where I had coaches who took us to meet professional baseball players like Frank Thomas, back when he was the most popular player in Chicago. My same coaches recommended me to take two summer courses with NFTE – National Foundation for Teaching Entrepreneurship, which helped me develop my entrepreneur mindset. I have to thank coach Kevin Kalinich, Steve Bridges, Kyle,

Craig and all the other coaches from the Bakongo little league baseball team. You might all know the movie "Hardball", that was based off of our team.

Then as time passed, I met Mr. Muhammad in High School who showed me multiple life principles that enhanced my thinking and expanded my wisdom through reading. It is definitely true when we say that it takes a village to raise a child. Even today I have two more mentors Reginald Grand'Pierre and Stacey Brown who have helped me master another level of success "Family".

Take advantage of every program that is offered to you and look for older mentors who truly want you to succeed and grow. All you have to do is listen, put in the work and have faith. Once again I wish you much success, stay positive and the world is yours.

– Diamond McNulty

<u>NOTES</u>

CHAPTER 10 REVIEW

1. The _____ you are the less painful things are mentally and physically.

2. You should always have a _____ for when you become successful.

3. Surround yourself with _____ that will keep you in line with your goals.

Repeat After Me

I am beautiful!

I am confident!

I can do anything I put my mind to!

I can become anything I want to become!

I will work hard and pursue my dreams!

I will earn my success!

I will never give up!

I will be successful!

The Success Plan

In this portion of the book we will assist you in starting your journey to "Becoming A Successful Young Woman".

For the full success plan, please purchase the How To Become A Successful Young Woman workbook at:

www.SuccessfulYoungWoman.com

THE VISION BOARD

"Taking Over The World"

As an initial step in developing a success plan, you will need to create a vision board. I want you to go to your nearest store and pickup (1) dry erase board, (1) dry board erase marker, (1) poster board and (1) map of the world. You will also need to collect some old newspaper and magazines.

Next, I want you to answer each question below on the dry erase board and place it on your wall to hang in your room. With the poster board you can either write on your board the things you want to accomplish or stick pictures of the things you want to accomplish to it and place it somewhere in your room so you can see it every day. Also, place the map of world in a place you can view every day as well.

1. What do you want to be in life?

Doctor, lawyer, Political Figure, Entrepreneur, Sports Owner, etc....

2. Name 2 backup plans?

3. What do you want to accomplish in your lifetime?

Your own company, A House, Car,

Spouse, Recognition

4. How will you make a difference in society? Give back to the youth? Become a Volunteer, mentor, donate?

5. Name every material thing you want? Price?

6. Name every material thing you need to accomplish your goals? Price?

(Clothes, Computer, Gadgets, TVs, Piano, Etc....)

7. What steps do you need to take to achieve your goals?

8. What schools will you attend? College? Graduate School Etc....?

9. What are the best places to do internships for your career?

Places you would love to travel?

Hobbies you will like to acquire?

Write 3 books you would like to read.

ABOUT THE AUTHORS

Mercedes Woodberry was born and raised in different areas including, Chicago's Robert Taylor Projects and Baton Rouge's Valley Park. She was surround by violence, gangs, drugs, and poverty. Although mistakes have been made, Mercedes Woodberry has proven that the impossible is very possible no matter the obstacles in your way or the cards you were dealt.

Mercedes Woodberry has undergone all of the trials and triumphs from jail, expulsion from school, playing the mother role for her siblings while her single parent was at work, running away, drug offers, physical abuse, verbal abuse and teen pregnancy. Still, like a phoenix she rose from the ashes.

Mercedes Woodberry is currently a Criminal Justice Degree holder, Federal Special Agent in the Army Criminal Investigations Command, Fitness Instructor, a student at University of Maryland, a Non-Commissioned Officer, an Author, and most importantly a SUCCESSFUL Young Woman.

For more details go to:

www.MercedesWoodberry.com

Diamond McNulty was born and raised in the Cabrini Green housing projects on the North side of Chicago, Illinois. Surrounded by gang violence, drugs and minimal opportunities, McNulty has achieved what many people believe to be 'The Impossible'. Dealing with various obstacles, he has created a system for success despite the cards he had been dealt. It goes to say that in order to gain it all, you must lose it all. The one thing that McNulty grasped that many kids don't at their age is the ability to listen and pay attention.

Leaving Chicago with $200 in his

pocket, all McNulty had were a boatload of expenses, student loans and a dream. His journey took hard work, faith, motivation, persistence and patience over the years to overcome what many believe to be the ultimate struggle. By winning various scholarships, teaching cooking classes, and mentoring kids, McNulty has dedicated his life to giving kids the knowledge it takes to become successful.

Through every struggle, McNulty embraced his experience as an opportunity to learn and grow. He surrounded himself with people like himself and learned the difference between gambling and investing. By traveling from city to city by himself, he set his goals and executed them one day at a time. McNulty worked 3 jobs around the clock in order to pay for college and start up his first 4 companies. He continues to grow into a prominent individual in society. McNulty is very grateful for every mentor that has entered his life and kept him on the right path along his journey to "Take Over The World".

Diamond McNulty is currently the CEO of McNulty International and Corporate Executive Chef of Taste of Diamond

Catering.

For more details go to:

www.DiamondMcnulty.com

The world is full of average people…

Be Great!

80271731R00104

Made in the USA
Columbia, SC
15 November 2017